What Everyone Needs to Know About Sex Addiction

CompCare Publishers

Minneapolis, Minnesota 55441

Library of Congress Cataloging-in-Publication Data

What everyone needs to know about sex addiction / Anonymous.
    p.   cm.
    Includes first-person stories from Hope and Recovery (Minneapolis, Minn.:
CompCare Publishers, ©1987)
    Bibliography: p.
    ISBN 0-89638-171-4:$4.95
    1. Sexual addiction—Popular works. I. Hope and Recovery.
II. Title.
RC560.S43A56   1989
616.85'83—dc20   89-10031
                                                                      CIP

Cover design by Jeremy Gale
Interior design by Lillian Svec

Inquiries, orders, and catalog requests should be addressed to:
CompCare Publishers
2415 Annapolis Lane
Minneapolis, MN 55441
Call toll free 800/328-3330
(Minnesota residents, 612/559-4800)

    5   4   3   2   1
    93   92   91   90   89

Contents

A Note To The Reader

Sex Addiction. Sex Addicts. Codependency. Less than ten years ago, these terms were all but unknown to the general population. When first introduced through research reports and publications, the words themselves and the concepts they represent startled many people and precipitated controversy within the treatment community.

Following publication of two of the first books on sex addiction, *Out of the Shadows* (1983) and *Hope and Recovery* (1987), more people began to respond to and acknowledge the concepts of sex addiction and codependency; subsequently, more people began to recognize these problems as authentic, serious, and life-affecting. But despite the fact that growing numbers of people acknowledge sex addiction and codependency, the concepts are still obscured by controversy and misunderstanding.

In an effort to create new understanding among the general population about the sensitive and still controversial subjects of sex addiction and codependency, we turned to people who shared their personal stories of addiction and recovery in the landmark book *Hope and Recovery.* We asked two of these people to share their stories in a brief, informational format that would be appropriate for use by the general public. The result is this book. It is worth noting that the original title for this work was *Our Struggle.* That first title is significant because the two people whose stories are included here are married to each other. And, in the course of their lives and their relationship, they *have* struggled—he with sex addiction and she with codependency to sex addiction. Truly, what they share here are personal stories of the pain of addiction and codependency that evolve as genuine testimonials to the reality of recovery.

As we reviewed the written material submitted by this couple, we realized that it contained essential information that *everyone* needs to know about sex addiction. In this time of heightened controversy about addiction—sex addiction in particular—it is important to us that this material helps clarify some important issues and offers basic information that is useful for anyone. Our belief is this: what everyone needs to know about sex addiction is represented by some simple but very important concepts, each addressed in this work by real people who have themselves struggled with and are recovering from sex addiction and codependency.

Like so many people who have, through the years, found help for their addictions, the couple who share their stories in this book credit their recovery to a Twelve Step Program based on Alcoholics Anonymous. You will note several references to the Twelve Step Program in this book. For further information about help and programs available, review A Message From The Authors and the recommended reading list on pages 43-46.

The Editors

Introduction

This book was written with three different kinds of readers in mind: (1) people who want to learn more about compulsive sexual behavior and codependency and how these problems affect real lives; (2) clergy, counselors, therapists, and other helping professionals who need a brief but effective method for educating their clients about compulsive sexual behavior and codependency; and (3) recovering sex addicts and codependents needing help for the process of making amends to those they have harmed.

History and literature document the fact that there have always been sex addicts in this world—people whose lives are shaped and driven by compulsive sexual behavior. And, throughout time, societal responses to these people have been dramatically varied. Some sex addicts have been proclaimed sinners and morally weak; some have been stoned to death in the village square. Some sex addicts have been feared and locked away in prisons; others have been pitied and called sick and perverted; still others have been "treated" with drugs, surgery, and electric shock. Some sex addicts have been joked about or ridiculed; some have been shamed. Some sex addicts have been worshipped; some have been regarded as heros and role models; other have been revered subjects of books and films. But rarely, if ever, have sex addicts been perceived or portrayed as people in pain. And, until quite recently, sex addicts were generally not viewed as driven, lonely, out of control people. Perhaps society did not want to believe that these people were out of control, just as sex addicts themselves do not want to believe that they are out of control in their thinking and behavior. But it is true: there are and always have been people—both men and women—who are addicted to sex, just as some people are addicted to alcohol or other drugs, or to overeating or gambling.

To a great extent, society as a whole still has difficulty acknowledging sex addiction, just as society had difficulty acknowledging alcoholism years ago. In the past fifty years, however, Alcoholics Anonymous (A.A.) has helped educate our society (including health care professionals) regarding addiction. With the help of A.A., millions of alcoholics are recovering. Only a few years ago, it was considered rather shameful—a fact thought worthy of secrecy—to have an alcoholic in a family. Now, in this society, alcoholism is understood to the degree that even prominent people have openly acknowledged their alcoholism, their need for help, and the fact that they are recovering. Seeing the effectiveness of A.A. in dealing with addiction, many sex addicts have adopted A.A.'s Twelve Step Program as a method of getting help for their painful, isolating problem.

Sex Addiction:
What is it?

"I knew for certain that I'd lose my job if I got arrested for picking up a prostitute. I had only one year left until retirement, but still I continued to risk *everything* by looking for prostitutes whenever time permitted. Every night after work, I'd be out cruising the streets. When I finally *was* arrested and booked, it seemed so unreal. But then, when the story hit the newspapers the next day, the reality was so painful that I considered suicide. I think the most difficult thing of all was going into the office during the weekend to clean out my desk. After nineteen years with the same company and many of the same coworkers, I left alone and in shame."

" 'Tramp,' 'slut,' 'whore,' 'nympho'—*I hated the names boys called me in high school. But their obvious lack of respect for me certainly didn't keep them from having sex with me. I hated myself and what I was doing. Finally, I just stopped having sex with* anyone *and I also stopped masturbating. I began dressing so that no one could see my body. I just shut down totally."*

"I used to wonder and worry what my family would think of me after I died: they'd go to clean out my house and find my terrible secret—a massive collection of hard-core pornography. The thought of my daughter going through my collection sickened me. Time after time, I had thrown out my collection, but then I always replaced it again before long."

"I honestly don't understand how it happened, but every time I'd go on a business trip out of town, I'd meet someone and we'd end up in bed together. I certainly don't remember planning these encounters or even really wanting them to occur. I always told myself that I didn't have to feel guilty because everyone had a few flings now and then and at least I hadn't planned mine; they just 'happened.' "

"I was pretty creative in making up excuses for why I didn't want to make love with my partner. How could I tell him that I was too sore from masturbating all day to have sex with him? I loved him, and I hated having this secret."

"I told myself that because I never touched anyone, my activity was really a 'victimless crime.' I even tried to tell myself that the people I flashed actually liked the experience. Oh sure, I said to myself, they act like they're afraid or angry, but deep down they really love it. I'm embarrassed to say that I used to tell myself those lies and I really believed them. I wish I had gotten help years ago."

"I'd be a very rich man today if I had a dime for every minute of my life I spent sitting in the bushes, waiting, and peeking in windows. Instead, I've wasted *years* of my life just hoping to catch a brief glimpse of someone undressing or having sex. All those lonely nights waiting and watching . . . I just wish I had that time back."

"Each time I came out of a porno movie or a strip show, I'd brace myself for the possibility of being seen by a member of my congregation. How would I ever explain my attendance at a sex show on Saturday night, particularly in light of my sermons on the evils of pornography on Sunday mornings? I kept praying that I'd be able to stop doing this, to stop living a lie. What had I done to deserve this hell on earth?"

"Spring was always the worst time. When the warm weather first arrived, everyone would be wearing shorts or bathing suits again after months in heavier clothing. I was so excited to see bodies again, I didn't pay attention to my driving at all. I'd slow down for a better look at people or drive around and around the block to get a second, third, or fourth look at someone. Sometimes I was so busy looking at bodies I'd completely forget what time it was and arrive two or three hours late for work. It's amazing that I never had—or caused—a major car accident."

———

The foregoing quotes from people of both sexes, various ages, and dissimilar backgrounds illustrate obsessive thinking and compulsive sexual behavior—the "acting out" characteristic of sex addiction. It's true to say that the problem of sex addiction can and does affect all kinds of people—regardless of age, sex, sexual orientation, socioeconomic background, religious background, or profession.

Some sex addicts act out their addictions alone, isolated from others; other sex addicts act out publically. But regardless of the nature or circumstances of the acting-out behaviors, one thing is common to all sex addicts: compulsive sexual behaviors and/or obsessive sexual thoughts *demand* their attention and eventually shape and control their lives. Acting-out behaviors become the focus of the sex addict's day. As with other addictions, sex addiction eventually relegates everything else in a person's life to "second place"—or less—after the addictive urge. Families, friends, careers, hobbies, education, and financial security are all placed in jeopardy as the addict relentlessly seeks the experience that he or she thinks will, at last, provide the ultimate high and subsequent peace from compulsion. But the high, once achieved, is never enough for the addicted person. Even as the sex addict is engaged in the very behavior that held promise for a new high, he or she begins to focus on the next high, its promise and details.

Like most addicted people, sex addicts often make solemn and believable promises that they will stop or in some way curtail their acting-out behaviors. And these promises are usually made in earnest to all of the right people: to themselves; to their loved ones; to their employers; to their lawyers; to their therapists; and to their God. But when addiction is a factor, even a sworn promise will soon be compromised, qualified, or completely broken—regardless of the sincerity with which it was made. Active addicts cannot say *no* to the object of their addiction for long. And if, by chance, one acting-out behavior is modified, curtailed, or stopped completely, another acting-out behavior is likely to take its place in a relatively short period of time.

Given the powerlessness of the addict, he or she is essentially compelled to act out at any cost. And the cost of sex addiction can be enormous—financially, physically, and emotionally. Some sex addicts spend large sums of money for sexual material or experiences; other sex addicts spend large sums of money to cover up the *consequences* of their addiction. The acting-out behaviors of some sex addicts lead to unwanted pregnancies and abortions, venereal diseases, and even death. The time that many sex addicts spend away from families, friends, and interests in pursuit of new sexual highs cannot be retrieved. The cost to one's self-respect and reputation is not measurable. And the final cost of sex addiction can be loss of sanity, a point at which some sex addicts believe that suicide would be easier than continuing to live a life that is driven by addiction.

Following is the story of one man's personal struggle with sex addiction:

Frank's Story: A Sex Addict's Struggle

I share my own story here to explain sex addiction in the most effective way I know how: as it operates in and affects the lives of real people in real-life situations. Clearly evident in my story and common to the stories of all sex addicts are the patterns of behavior and thinking best described as powerlessness and unmanageability. These behavior and thought patterns essentially controlled my life every day of my life for more than a decade.

My story would not be complete without including both positive and painful realities of my recovery; I have now been recovering from sex addiction for more than four years. I owe my recovery, and therefore my life, to the Twelve Step Program that helped me break an addiction that shaped, controlled, and almost destroyed my life.

I believe that my addiction started when I was eleven years old. I remember that there was always a great deal of pain in our family. My father traveled frequently and my mother hated the town we lived in. I remember being told that I was different from other kids in town and that I'd have to be the man of the house whenever my father was gone. When my father *was* home, he was always fighting with my mother. In a desperate attempt to avoid the fighting, I finally worked out an escape plan: I'd go into the bathroom, lock the door, and take a bath. I spent *hours* locked in that bathroom, hiding from the world outside; it was there that I first discovered masturbation. My discovery was very exciting to me because it helped me forget the pain and loneliness I struggled with outside that tiny room.

I quickly developed an addictive behavior pattern around masturbation: I'd set my alarm clock so that I'd have some extra time to masturbate before school in the morning; I'd even go to bed early at night so that I'd have plenty of time to masturbate before I fell asleep. At that time in my life, I had no access to pornographic materials, so I spent hours looking through mail-order catalogs for photographs of women in lingerie. Almost right away, I set some arbitrary rules to control my sexual behavior. For example, I'd tell myself that I could masturbate to only one photograph per page. Even then, I sensed that if I *didn't* set some rules, I'd lose control and masturbate at the sight of every picture on every page. Early on, I decided that masturbating and looking at photographs for sexual pleasure *must* be wrong, because no one else talked about doing such things. I continued to enjoy this little diversion of mine, even though I sensed it was wrong. By the time I was thirteen, I was masturbating five times a day and desperately wanting to be sexual with girls. I didn't have a certain girl in mind, I just wanted to be sexual with someone, *anyone.* I went out with girls my own age when I first started dating, but I soon discovered that these girls didn't respond to the pressure I put on them to be sexual with me. While other young people my age were giggling about holding hands, I was fantasizing about oral sex. Now, when I look back on those years, I realize that I missed out on so much innocent discovery and joy because of my obsession with sex.

Because I matured early and looked much older than my chronological age, I started seeking out older girls when I was only fourteen years old. At that time, in fact, I looked and acted old enough so that I could buy liquor. I intentionally started hanging around with older boys who had cars so that I'd be able to expand my search for girls. When I was unable to get a ride from someone, I'd just hitchhike to other towns and look for girls. Soon I had a sex partner in each town I visited. I had always assumed that masturbation and pornography would lose their appeal for me as soon as I had my first sexual experience with a girl. But when I lost my virginity at the age of fourteen, my obsessions became even more powerful. In addition to masturbating every day, I would have sex with one or more girls every day. By the time I was in my early teens, I was already using sex to deal with my feelings and my problems. I'd masturbate when I was lonely, confused, anxious, happy, sad, angry, scared, or tired. Whatever the problem, I truly believed that masturbation would somehow solve it, or at least make me feel better. As soon as I turned sixteen, I bought a car of my own so that I'd be able to search for sexual partners in an even larger geographic area.

I didn't have many male friends when I was a teenager. I discovered that most boys my age were not particularly interested in spending all day talking about sex and all night *looking* for it. And, of course, other boys were often angry with me because I had tried to have sex with their girlfriends. When I was fifteen years old, a male schoolteacher initiated a sexual relationship with me. This man would give me "gifts" whenever I visited him at his home. I was not attracted to him sexually, but I did like the attention and gifts he gave me; actually, I felt powerless to refuse his requests. I kept telling myself that I really had no reason to be intimidated by this teacher, and that it was sophisticated and hip to be sexual with women *and* men. Nevertheless, I was always terribly afraid that someone would find out about my sexual relationship with this man.

During my teenage years, my mother's friends often commented about how cute I was and how sexy I looked in my tight blue jeans. I enjoyed all the praise I got from these adult women. It somehow seemed like an affirmation of my manhood to get this kind of attention from married women, yet I felt sick to my stomach each time one of them hugged me, rubbed up against me, or even touched me.

I got a job when I was a teenager in order to pay for car expenses and all of the condoms I was using. It just so happened that I went to work in a store that employed a number of women. Subsequently, I had sex with as many of my female coworkers as possible. Most of these women had more money than I had, and some of them bought me liquor or gave me "gifts" of money after I had sex with them. In the course of having dozens of sexual encounters with married women, I began putting myself in potentially dangerous situations. Oftentimes, I'd arrange to have sex with women in their homes while their husbands were at work. When I visited a woman whose husband had a long history of drinking and violence, I'd *tell* myself that my sweaty palms, rapid heartbeat, and shallow breathing were just signs of sexual excitement, not fear at the thought that I might be discovered and maybe even *killed*. (This was not the first or last time during my acting-out days that I would confuse fear with excitement.)

I began to suspect that other people didn't live the way I did. But when I talked about my obsessions and behaviors with the few friends I had, they assured me that I didn't have a problem. In fact, some people told me that I was living out every man's dream. *But these people didn't hear the loneliness in my voice.* I concluded that my life would settle down when I found the right woman. I wasn't sure how I'd find her, because I was spending almost all of my time with older, married women. And when I *did* spend time with women my own age, that often led to my having sex with their sisters, their cousins, and sometimes even their mothers. During this time, I frequently was sexual with people I didn't respect or even *like*. But none of this mattered as long as I could have sex with someone; *any sacrifice was worth it.*

I started picking up women in bars and ultimately contracted venereal disease. I was so completely out of control by this time that I actually tried to pick up a woman while both of us waited in line for medication at a V.D. clinic. I was relatively isolated at school because almost everyone knew of my obsession with sex. I was also filled with rage, and this rage seemed to manifest itself when I was being sexual with women. In fact, one time I was so violent with a woman when she refused to have sex with me that I broke her leg. I was *terrified* about my behavior and completely out of control. I finally turned to drugs in a desperate attempt to "mellow" out. It's probably not surprising that I used drugs in the same compulsive way that I had used sex—everywhere, all the time. I'd get high on drugs before school, in school, and after school as well. The drugs "worked" in that they slowed me down for a while, but I realized that I always made a fool of myself when I was high. I knew I'd have to choose between sex and drugs. This choice was really quite easy for me because I knew that no woman wanted to have sex with a fool.

Somehow, in the midst of all this acting-out behavior, I managed to establish a relationship with a woman I had admired for a long time. When we started dating, I promised myself that I wouldn't be sexual with her; I wasn't going to let sex interfere with this promising new relationship. At first, I *did* abstain from having sex with this woman and I even reduced the number of other sex partners in my life. (I lied to her and told her I was not sexually involved with anyone else.) But it didn't take me long to realize that my theory was wrong: finding the right woman was *not* the solution to my problems with compulsive sexual behavior.

Thinking that I needed a fresh start, I chose to go away to college; my girlfriend went away to college in another town. By the time we went our separate ways to school, we were engaged and planned to get married after we graduated. Because of my new start in college and my plans for marriage, I promised myself that I would not be sexual with anyone while I was away at school, and *I really meant it.* But even though I fully intended to honor this promise, I lost control immediately. When I felt lonely on my *first night away at school,* I dealt with those feelings of loneliness by being sexual with someone. Just a couple weeks later, I had fully resumed my compulsive behavior pattern: I'd have sex with five different women during the week, then spend weekends with my fiancée.

I was so afraid of getting someone pregnant that I had a vasectomy when I was only eighteen years old. My fiancée wanted us to be sexual, but because of my experiences with other women, I was fearful that a sexual encounter between us would *destroy* our relationship. I also feared that I'd completely lose control of my behavior once I started being sexual with her. In fact, I was so afraid of being sexual with her that the first time we made love, I completely blanked out and had no real sense of what was going on. Once I had sex with my fiancée, I lost the last excuse I had for my compulsive behavior. No longer could I say, "I'll stop messing around when I finally have the opportunity to be sexual with my fiancée." Realizing that I had no more excuses for my compulsive behavior and wanting to spare this young woman any additional pain, I ended our relationship. I was too ashamed to tell her the *real* reason I was ending our relationship, so I lied to her and said I didn't love her anymore. It was very painful for me to end this relationship. And the best, most reliable way I could think of to numb that pain was to be sexual with other women as often as possible. Now that I was a "free" man again, I was somewhat relieved to know that I would no longer have to feel guilty about being unfaithful to my fiancée.

One of the women I was sexual with while I was engaged seemed to me the "perfect" woman, perhaps the woman I'd been searching for in all of my sexual encounters. Jean seemed to enjoy sex as much as I did and, furthermore, she was willing to do anything of a sexual nature that I suggested. I couldn't *imagine* having a better relationship. I was sure that the pain I was still feeling would go away as our commitment to each other grew stronger. Jean and I had sex whenever we could. For example, instead of studying at the library, we'd find a private room there and fondle one another as we read. Looking back, I can see so clearly that whenever I was confused or frustrated about my studies, I'd immediately want to be sexual. Rather than working through my feelings, I avoided them *completely* by engaging in sex. Jean and I engaged in sexual activities so often that I didn't even have time to be sexual with other women. Together, we tried something new and invited other women to be sexual with us. We subsequently lost many friends who would not tolerate our constant references to sex and the fact that we propositioned friends and strangers.

Our frenetic sexual activity with other people continued until we both graduated from college and moved into an apartment. We found it much more difficult to locate sex partners after we moved off campus, so we began advertising for them in newspapers. Ultimately, these advertisements resulted in my having sexual encounters with men. Now *everyone* was a potential sex partner for me. Jean and I began going to bars, picking up women, taking them home, and then photographing them in the underwear we collected. I'd tell myself that this life I was leading was the *good life*—not every man was lucky enough to have a woman who'd *help* him pick up sex partners and apply makeup to the nude models he photographed. In addition to the group sex Jean and I participated in, we began to vary our sexual activity with each other: we engaged in bondage and sadomasochism and we also began acting out our violent fantasies. Once we started doing these things, I was afraid *not* to continue, for fear that Jean would decide that I was boring and leave me. At the same time, I was afraid that I might begin to *enjoy* the new things we were doing. I didn't discuss my fears and confusion with *anyone*. People often told me that I had it made, but I knew the truth: *I was completely out of control and I was abusing myself and others as well.* I blamed myself for corrupting Jean. As much as I cared about her, I honestly hoped that she'd realize what was happening, end the relationship, and just leave me to my masturbation and pornography.

When I finished graduate school and got a job as a counselor, my double life really began to take hold. I spent my days helping other people break their addictions to drugs and I spent my nights acting out my own addiction. *I hated myself for being such a hypocrite.* When I began to notice striking similarities between my sexual behavior and the addictive behavior of my clients in relation to chemical use, I could see that I was addicted to sex. In an attempt to stop acting out sexually, I attended meetings of A.A. (Alcoholics Anonymous). But

I quickly discovered that I could not *lie* my way into a Program that is built on a foundation of honesty and truth. The people in the A.A. group I attended accepted me and welcomed me, but I found that I was unable to accept myself or their fellowship because of my fear of opening up and telling my sexual secrets. *I decided that I was, indeed, addicted to sex but that no one else had an addiction quite like mine. I believed that no one would understand my problem.* At that point, I resigned myself to a long and miserable life, because it seemed that my energies were tied up either in acting out or in struggling to not act out.

When I no longer had the energy to even go out socially, Jean began going out alone. One night she came home and told me that she had spent some time with another man and had really enjoyed herself. Finally, I could see the end of our relationship coming. I knew that no one else would want me in the emotional, mental, and spiritual condition I was in at that time. I decided to take care of the mess that my life had become by killing myself. For some reason, though, I felt I owed it to my profession to at least call a suicide-prevention hot line before I took my life. This call, I felt, would constitute the perfect end to my life. The man who answered my hot line call was evidently inexperienced and/or improperly trained, because he put me on "hold" after I told him of my desperation. In response, I flew into a rage and smashed the window of the phone booth I was standing in. I vowed to overcome my addiction just to spite this insensitive person on the phone and whatever kind of God would allow my life to disintegrate in this way.

I stopped being sexual with almost everyone but Jean, but the passion was gone from our sex. Both of us were there for each other *physically,* but absent emotionally. I began to masturbate more often, making regular promises to myself that I quickly broke: "I'll only masturbate ten times today"; "I'll never masturbate at work"; "I'll never sink so low as to use that kind of pornography." My penis ached and my ejaculations no longer gave me any sense of pleasure or release. *Again, I was driven and out of control.* What would it take for me to stop? I often wondered if losing Jean or my job would make me stop acting out. I was already losing my sanity, but *that* realization hadn't been enough to motivate me to change. Then one day, as if by accident, another sex addict told me that I was not alone in my sex addiction. He said that there were other men and women who had known firsthand the hell I was living in. But even more miraculous, he said, *these people had recovered; they had healed.* He told me incredible stories about people who were no longer driven, people who could be faithful to their lovers, live sane and healthy lives, *and be happy doing so.* I told this man that I would settle for not being driven; happiness seemed too much to hope for. Before I went to my first Twelve Step meeting for sex addicts, I vacillated between thinking I'd be the only person at the meeting with any intelligence or class, and thinking that they may not even allow me into the group because I was so sick. In either case, I knew the people in this group wouldn't be like me because I was different. As it turned out, the other sex addicts at the meeting were more *like* me than *unlike* me. The one thing we all had in common was the one thing that really mattered: we were sex addicts. But still I was afraid—afraid that the Twelve Steps might not work for me and that I'd *never* recover. At the same time, I was afraid that the Twelve Steps *would* work for me and I'd have to give up my acting-out behaviors forever. Neither option seemed very pleasant. *I wondered who I'd be if I stopped acting out.* I had worked hard to establish and keep the reputation I had. In fact, being a sex addict was my identity, my personality. My whole life revolved around sex and I was convinced that I'd be nothing at all without it. The way I dressed, my humor, my priorities—everything in my life revolved around my compulsive sexual behavior. *How could I possibly let go of all that?*

With the help of this Twelve Step group, I set my boundaries and called my sponsor every week, just as I was supposed to do. And I didn't act out. *At least I didn't act out until I got really lonely.* Rather than calling my group sponsor one time, I acted out instead. I told myself it wasn't such a big deal because I couldn't possibly get caught. It wasn't as if I'd broken the law, or been arrested, or lost my job. I had merely broken a commitment to myself one time and one time only. I had absolutely no intention of telling the group about my slip; I'd *never* get a medallion marking my time in recovery without a slip. I just knew I wouldn't be able to live the rest of my life without acting out. I told myself that I was much better than I *had* been, and that I had at least *some* control over my behavior. But for some reason, this self-talk *just didn't ring true to me.* I sat through the whole first half of a meeting before I told the other group members about my slip. They immediately reassured me that it was okay—that slips happen to almost everyone at one time or another and that I was welcome to continue coming to meetings. But then, one person in the group spoke directly to me and said, "I still accept you, Frank, but if you're ever going to get better *you'll have to be true to yourself.*" His words echoed in my head and I *hated* him for what he said. Who did he think he was to tell me what to do?

Before long, the stresses of life got to me and I sought out my old friend—pornography. It happened that my supply of pornographic material was there in the closet, right where I had put it, *just in case.* I decided to look at it and *not* masturbate. But once I got back into the addictive cycle, I was completely powerless again. As I unsuccessfully tried to ejaculate, the words I'd heard at my last group meeting were still ringing in my head. Finally, I burned the pornography, just as I had done so many times in the past. But this time, I did something different after burning my supply of pornography: I called another sex addict on the phone. This time I told him what was *really* going on with me, how lonely and afraid I was, and how I desperately wanted to continue acting out. This man told me to pray. I didn't know what to pray *for* or who to pray *to,* so I just admitted my powerlessness over this addiction over and over again. I was so angry about being an addict. Tears streamed down my checks as I pounded the walls and screamed. "Help me!" I cried.

I prayed for a bolt of lightning or the voice of God to come into the room, but nothing happened—nothing except for the fact that *I did not act out that day.* After this incident, I suddenly had several new opportunities to act out: my first sponsor left the Program and started acting out again himself; Jean moved out; people I'd had sexual encounters with in the past showed up at my door; and publishers of pornographic magazines continued to send copies of their materials to me, even after I wrote and told them to remove my name from their mailing lists. But through all these circumstances and changes, I managed to stay true to myself and I did not act out.

When I was acting out, I had always "sexualized" my emotions. This is to say I had always assumed that whatever I was feeling, that feeling meant that I had a need to be sexual; I continued to have problems with this sexualization of my feelings, even in recovery. Then I developed a close relationship with another member of the Twelve Step group I attended. I respected this man for his ability to use the Twelve Steps, as well as for his wisdom, his humor, and the fact that he seemed to genuinely *like* himself. I often thought about him sexually, even during meetings. I'd drop hints as we spoke and I'd try to establish eye contact with him while he was sharing with the group. One evening, after our regular group meeting had ended and some of us were getting ready to go out for a meal together, I saw my opportunity to have some time alone with this man. I asked him if I could ride to the restaurant with him and he agreed. When we were in the car, I started talking about how I wasn't really sure if I was heterosexual or homosexual. I told him that even though most of my acting-out behaviors had occurred with women, I considered the possibility that I might be gay and perhaps needed to learn to be comfortable with that fact. He pointed out to me that sex addiction is not about *who* a person acts out with but *why* that person acts out at all. *This man just wouldn't take the hint I was giving him.* I tried again: I told him that what I thought I *really* needed was a loving, gentle relationship with a man—a relationship that would help me decide, once and for all, whether or not I was homosexual. He said, "I agree that you need loving and gentle relationships with men, Frank, and I would be honored to be one of those men." I was overjoyed when he said this and fully expected that we'd skip dinner and go straight to his apartment for sex. But as he began speaking again, I realized that wasn't what he had in mind at all. "Right now," he said, "it really doesn't matter if you're gay or not. All that matters is your recovery. You don't have to consider your sexual orientation until you're more secure in your recovery and you're not acting out anymore. I care about you, and I won't endanger your recovery or mine by being sexual with you. You need to learn to love and be loved by other men without having those relationships involve sex. I can care about you and want to be with you without wanting to have sex with you." *I didn't know what to do.* The concept of caring deeply for someone *without* sexual involvement seemed so radical, so completely *unnatural* to me. I decided that this man must have said what he did because he really didn't like me and didn't *want* to be sexual with me. *He was putting me off.* For most of my life, I assumed that I had to give my body to someone for him or her to be willing to spend time with me. After spending more time in recovery, I would come to understand that this man had gently taught me a very important lesson about real intimacy.

When I finally told Jean that I was a sex addict, she was furious with me. I expected that she'd immediately break off our relationship, but she didn't. What surprised me most, though, was that she was more angry about my masturbation than she was about my sexual encounters with other women. Later on, she explained this reaction: she figured that if she satisfied me sexually and was willing to engage in sex with me whenever I wanted, she'd actually be able to *control* my addiction. It seemed that the healthier I became, the more confused she became about my addiction and our relationship. This time, *I* was the one who considered ending the relationship.

Fortunately, Jean got into a Twelve Step Program of her own—one organized especially for codependent people. But our relationship continued to be a struggle, even when both of us were getting help and getting better. There were so many changes in the ways we interacted with each other: we were fighting a lot and we often abstained from sexual activity with each other. During these times of change, we often wondered if there was more to our relationship than sex and sickness, and whether or not recovery was worth losing each other. After more than a year of struggling together, we decided to make a statement to ourselves and the world regarding the important changes in our relationship: we got married. People from our respective Twelve Step groups came to the wedding, supported us, and celebrated with us as we made a commitment to each other.

As Jean and I struggled with the challenges of a new marriage, I was still struggling with my addiction. I continued to play games with the boundaries I had set. For example, I'd quantify and qualify masturbation in an effort to make it something other than acting out behavior (". . . *only once a week*"; "*only every third time I really get the urge*"; ". . . *only if I don't think about anyone but my wife*"; ". . . *only if I don't think about sex at all*"; and on and on). I finally realized that anything I had to have so many rules around *must* be addictive. I finally admitted to myself, my group, and my God that masturbation was addictive behavior for me. My acting-out behavior had actually *numbed* my emotions and I had mistaken every feeling I had for a sexual urge.

I recall that at one Twelve Step group meeting a man who had been very important to my early recovery announced that he was leaving our group to meet with another one; he was doing this simply because the other group met at a time more convenient for him. One by one, each person in our group said good-bye to this man and thanked him for his help. When my turn came, *I had no words* and I began to weep. I went to him and he held me as I cried. My tears actually said more than any words, because this man knew how hard it was for me to cry and to trust other men.

Another milestone in my recovery occurred at a group meeting when I was telling my personal story: I actually *experienced* my emotions for the first time. I had told the facts many times before, but felt nothing. There was nothing special about this particular meeting—as always, our group consisted of five men sitting in a church basement, trying to help each other. But when I told my story on this particular night, I didn't just talk about my pain; *I really felt the pain.* For the first time, I realized how lonely, hurt, and shame-filled I had been and still was. I had always considered only the anger—never the sadness, the fear, or other emotions. I *hated* what I was feeling that night and was concerned that other people in the group might think that I was weak. Feeling as low and worthless as I did, it was so hard to trust that these people still cared about me.

Not all of the emotions I have gotten in touch with through recovery are painful to me. For example, I have discovered my laugh—not the little smile and chuckle I had when I was acting out, but a noisy, fun, belly laugh! Sometimes newcomers to meetings wonder how we can laugh and joke with each other, but they soon learn that a certain amount of levity is an essential part of the process of learning to be comfortable with other people and learning to care about them.

Now I realize that in recovery, I have everything I was trying to achieve by acting out: friends, acceptance, affection, and spirituality. I still don't know how to adequately explain spirituality; I do know what it is *not.* For me, spirituality is not standing back from life or refusing to enjoy it. Now I know how and what to pray about at night and during the day as well. I pray for the willingness to continue to work the Twelve Steps and the knowledge of which spiritual path to take. I end each day with a prayer of gratitude for my recovery—even at the end of a day when things didn't go my way. *Even my worst day in recovery is better than the best day I had while I was acting out.*

Postscript: Just a few months after writing my story, I had a slip that proved to be a very valuable lesson for me. When I first became involved in my Twelve Step group, I was there for *me*. I hurt so much at that time and I wanted to recover more than I wanted anything else. I was willing to give up *whatever* I'd have to give up for recovery. I figured that I would lose Jean and maybe my job, but I knew that any sacrifice would be worth it if I could just stop acting out and stop hating myself so much. After my first full year of not acting out, I figured that this recovery process wasn't so difficult after all. I had been active in my Twelve Step fellowship and felt that I was liked and respected by others. In the meantime, Jean and I got married and I established my career.

Suddenly, the pain of my early days in recovery seemed very distant to me. I was much less concerned about missing meetings or forgetting my reading and my prayers than I had been early in my recovery. I decided that I didn't need to continue calling another addict each day. By the time I got my two-year medallion marking two years of recovery without a slip, I was no longer working a *personal* recovery program at all. I wasn't acting out, but I wasn't truly at peace with myself either. I was fantasizing in many of the same ways I had fantasized *before* I came to the Program. I still attended meetings, but I didn't talk about *myself* very much. I was far too busy helping others and trying to look good. I made phone calls to other sex addicts, but only to see how *they* were doing. I never mentioned to anyone the struggle I was having again with my *own* addictive urges; I felt sure I could handle things by myself after the two good years I'd had in recovery. After all, I hadn't acted out during that time. If things got bad then, I'd just call someone. *I knew I couldn't act out anymore.* What would my group say if they found out? What would Jean do if she found out? I felt sure that these questions alone, and the fears they represented, would prevent me from acting out.

Then, one day I acted out. But before I did, I considered the option of calling someone from my group and *not* acting out. I decided not to call anyone. After my slip, I gave myself a *hundred* reasons why I would not have to call my behavior "acting out"—even though my behavior was clearly outside the boundaries I had set for myself in recovery. *I didn't call anyone from the group.* I was afraid I'd lose control and continue acting out. I didn't lose control, so I thought to myself: Well, this just proves I can go back to doing what I want to do now because I've got everything under control.

After my slip, I went to my group meeting as usual and told the people there how well my recovery was proceeding. I even comforted another addict and offered him some suggestions when he told me about a recent slip *he'd* had. I found that as the meeting continued on, I struggled more and more with my own reality. I invented more reasons why I wouldn't have to call what I had done acting-out behavior. I was feeling so anxious, I was afraid that I might throw up right there at the meeting. Suddenly, I realized that I couldn't sit still any longer and I blurted out my admission: "I had a slip last week!" I fully expected the men in the group to gasp in shock or move away from me in disgust when I revealed my secret. I waited for someone to tell me how I had let everyone down by lying to the group, but I heard none of the horrible things I was braced for. Instead, I heard only expressions of acceptance and support from people in the group. *I was honest and it paid off.* As a result, I felt as though an enormous weight had been lifted from my shoulders.

Today, I really work my Twelve Step Program. I have learned that a medallion marking the amount of time in recovery without a slip is not the goal of the Program, but merely a symbol of *progress* in the Program. I no longer mark on my calendar when I'll get my next medallion, because there is no way I can really know that for sure. I *do* know that I *am* a sex addict and that I *am* powerless over my compulsive sexual behavior. I can't promise that I will not act out next month or tomorrow; I only know that *I will not act out today.*

What has helped me most in my recovery is paying attention to the Twelve Steps and really applying them in my daily life. Being in therapy and also being a professional counselor, I am sometimes tempted to theorize and "therapize" in my Twelve Step meetings. But I have learned that I really get and give the best kind of help when I stay focused on the Twelve Steps. When I'm asked for help from another group member, I don't tell that person about the latest theoretical book I've read; instead, I tell that person about my experience and how I have used the Twelve Steps in my life. In fact, most newer group members don't even know what I do for a living. I am at the meetings only as another recovering sex addict, not as a trained helping professional. When I ask for help from other addicts, I don't ask them what they think their therapist would have to say about my problem; I ask them for suggestions as to how I can do a better job of applying the Twelve Steps to my daily life.

One of the most surprising things I have learned about myself in recovery is that I had actually been *afraid* of sex! (If someone had told me this during the years I was acting out, I would have said they were crazy.) Once I stopped fantasizing and began to pay attention to my body and my feelings *during* sex, I recognized the very real fear I had experienced around sex. The concept of healthy, gentle, loving sex is new for me and I'm just learning how to deal with it in my life. Now I am also learning how to be playful and joyful in my sexual relationship with my wife.

Another thing about my recovery that surprises me is that I rarely *want* to act out now. *Acting out has almost completely lost its appeal for me.* No longer can I fool myself into believing that pornography will help me be less lonely or that an affair will prove that I'm a good person. When I am in a very stressful situation, addictive thoughts still come into my mind. But now I know that I have group members to call; staying sober is no longer the terrible struggle for me that it was at first.

When I tell people that I no longer struggle with my addiction, some of them ask me if I'm permanently "cured." I don't feel that I'm "cured"; I believe that I will *always* be a sex addict. I used to feel sorry for myself and sometimes I felt anger for having to rely on a group to help me get through life. Now I feel grateful that I have a group of people who care enough about me that they want to see me each week and hear about my life and how it's going. I think of the piece of paper I carry with me, an important phone list that contains the phone numbers of the members of my Twelve Step group. I am moved when I consider the collect calls I've placed from faraway cities, calls that were accepted because these people understood what I was feeling and that I wanted to talk to another recovering addict. With people like this in my life, why would I want to stop attending meetings? I used to say that I *had* to go to Twelve Step meetings; now I find myself saying—and thinking—that I *get* to go to Twelve Step meetings. I don't struggle with my addiction anymore, but that doesn't mean I am recovered. I am proud and happy to say that I am a recover*ing* sex addict. The effort, pain, and time I invested in recovery has paid off in ways that I never would have believed possible.

Questions To Consider

As I shared my personal story of addiction with other sex addicts and they shared their stories with me, we all became acutely aware of similarities in our thinking, behaviors, and experiences. Drawing on these similarities, we developed the sixty-five questions that follow as a guide for other people who may wish to examine their own sexual thoughts and behaviors.

These questions do not constitute a standardized test or inventory designed to diagnose or evaluate addiction. Instead, these questions reflect our own experiences; our point is simply that those people who answer "yes" to a number of these questions have personal histories that are similar to ours. We hope that people who do respond affirmatively to these questions will carefully consider the impact that their sexual thoughts and behaviors have on their lives today. Those who have concerns about their sexual thoughts and behaviors need to know that, like us, they can find help and support through a Twelve Step Program.

☐   1. Do you sense that your sexual thoughts and/or behaviors are causing problems in your life?

☐   2. Have sexual thoughts interfered with your ability to function at work or at school?

☐   3. Do you worry that your sexual thoughts and/or behaviors are more powerful than you are?

☐   4. Do you sometimes think that you are the only person who has certain sexual thoughts or engages in certain sexual behaviors?

☐   5. Do you fail to meet commitments or fail to carry out responsibilities because of your sexual behaviors?

☐   6. Do you struggle to control or to completely stop your sexual thoughts and/or behaviors?

☐ 7. Do you fantasize about sex, or masturbate, or engage in sexual activity with another person in order to escape, deny, or numb your feelings?

☐ 8. Do you think about sex either more or less than you would like to?

☐ 9. Do you think of yourself as a person who has no sexual thoughts or desires whatsoever?

☐ 10. Do you think that there is something wrong or abnormal regarding the frequency of sexual activity that you have or wish to have?

☐ 11. Do you spend more money than you can afford to spend on sexual activities?

☐ 12. Does it seem as though there is another person or force inside of you that drives you to be sexual?

☐ 13. Do you have two standards of fidelity—one for yourself and one for your partner?

☐ 14. Do you think you would be happy if only you had enough sex and/or just the right sex partner(s)?

☐ 15. Do you feel empty or shameful after having sexual fantasies or engaging in sexual activity?

☐ 16. Do you feel obligated to have sex?

☐ 17. Have you ever promised yourself that you would never again have another sexual relationship?

☐ 18. Do you find it necessary to fantasize during sexual activity?

☐ 19. Do you set rules regulating the frequency of your sexual thoughts and activities?

☐ 20. Do you dress in such a way as to make your body appear undesirable?

☐ 21. Do you set rules regarding when, how, or with whom you can be sexual, then break those rules?

☐ 22. Do you use sexual thoughts and/or behaviors to deal with, deny, or avoid problems in your life?

☐ 23. Do you use threats or promises in order to have sexual activity with another person?

☐ 24. Do you sometimes find yourself being sexual or flirting with someone and wondering how it happened?

☐ 25. Do you risk legal problems in order to be sexual?

☐ 26. Have you stayed in a marriage or other relationship only because you thought that relationship somehow *protected* you from being promiscuous?

☐ 27. Do you think that your sexual abilities are the most important qualities you have to offer another person?

☐ 28. Are you fearful of seeking medical attention for injuries related to your sexual activities?

☐ 29. Do you anxiously anticipate or fear trips out of town because of what you think you might do sexually while you're away?

☐ 30. When you have child care responsibilities, do you put a higher priority on masturbating or being sexual than you do on the welfare of the child(ren) in your care?

☐ 31. Do your sexual thoughts and/or behaviors interfere with your spiritual or religious life? Do your sexual thoughts and/or behaviors cause you to believe that you don't *deserve* to have a religious or spiritual life?

☐ 32. Are you afraid to be left alone with children, for fear of being sexual with them?

☐ 33. Have your sexual thoughts and/or behaviors led you to consider suicide, castration, or self-mutilation?

☐ 34. When you are in a relationship with someone, do you try to make sure that another sex partner will be available to you in case anything goes wrong with the first relationship?

☐ 35. Do you stay in unsatisfying, painful, humiliating, or otherwise unhealthy relationships only so that you can continue to be sexual with someone?

☐   36. Do you spend time with people you don't even like or respect, hoping that you will have an opportunity to be sexual with them?

☐   37. Do you have sex with your partner even when he or she is ill?

☐   38. Does your sexual partner complain about your need for sex or your sexual behaviors? Does he or she refuse to participate in certain sexual activities with you?

☐   39. Do you either minimize or exaggerate the facts when discussing your sexual life with others?

☐   40. Have you ever tried to stop your sexual activity in an effort to end a painful relationship or behavior pattern?

☐   41. Do you initiate sexual activity with a partner before he or she is awake?

☐   42. Do you have chronic medical problems with your sex organs?

☐   43. Do you put yourself in danger by not taking reasonable precautions or by going to unsafe places in order to have sex?

☐   44. Have you lost a job or risked losing a job because of your sexual behaviors?

☐   45. Do your sexual behaviors cause you to violate the ethical standards, principles, and/or oaths of your profession?

☐   46. Do you scan printed material (novels, newspapers, magazines) or change channels on the television set just to find something that will stimulate you sexually?

☐   47. Do you regularly engage in fantasies involving self-abuse or other kinds of physical abuse?

☐   48. Do you trade material things (dinner, drugs, money) for sex?

☐ 49. Do your sexual behaviors lead you to risk injury, illness, or death?

☐ 50. Have your sexual behaviors led to treatment or hospitalization?

☐ 51. Do you masturbate after having sex?

☐ 52. Have you injured yourself due to the frequency, intensity, or nature of your masturbation or other sexual activities?

☐ 53. Would you rather masturbate than be sexual with a partner?

☐ 54. Do you spend time looking through windows, hoping that you might see something that will stimulate you sexually?

☐ 55. Do you follow people on the street, pick up hitchhikers, or drive around in your car, hoping that these activities will lead to sexual encounters?

☐ 56. Do you undress, masturbate, or engage in sexual activities in places where strangers are likely to see you?

☐ 57. Do you feel compelled to dress a certain way or to take part in certain rituals in order to masturbate or be sexual with another person?

☐ 58. Do you seek out crowds so that you can rub against people or otherwise be in close physical contact with strangers?

☐ 59. Do you make phone calls to strangers in order to talk about sex or masturbate?

☐ 60. Do you masturbate while driving?

☐ 61. Have you ever been sexual with animals?

☐ 62. Have you replaced a collection of pornographic material after destroying one collection and vowing never to purchase pornography again?

☐ 63. Do you masturbate or engage in sexual activity with partners in public places?

☐ 64. Do you steal money in order to engage in sexual activities?

☐ 65. Has an important relationship in your life ended because of your inability to stop being sexual outside of that relationship?

Codependency To Sex Addiction: An explanation

"I didn't want to see what was happening. I was too afraid, too ashamed. When the clues that he was having yet another extramarital affair became so obvious that I could no longer overlook them, I tried to make him end the affair. I threatened him; I blamed myself; I tried harder. But nothing I did seemed to work for very long."

"I used to think I was a prude because I really didn't want to try the new sexual activities my partner suggested. But I always cooperated and did whatever he asked. Never once did I stop to think about whether I really wanted to do these things or if they were even within my value system. I was terribly afraid that he'd be disappointed in me or leave me if I didn't satisfy him and go along with his suggestions."

"I thought she'd stop flirting with other men when we got married, but she didn't. I thought she'd stop watching those X-rated sex videos when we had our first child, but she didn't. I was always so preoccupied with her behavior when we went to parties together. I was in constant fear that she'd make an obvious sexual comment to someone and embarrass me or harm my chances for a promotion at work. I never knew whether she really was having sex with other men or just *talking* as if she had been unfaithful. I'm not sure I really *wanted* to know."

"Finally, I couldn't stand it anymore. I just went crazy! I started yelling and cursing him. I opened up the front door and began throwing all of his porno magazines out on the lawn. The neighbors must have thought I had lost my mind."

"I blamed myself for not being able to keep up with her excessive sexual demands. It wasn't just the fact that she wanted to have sex so often that concerned me, but that when we were having sex, it never seemed like we were making love. I wanted to feel close and loving, but her only interests were variety and frequency."

———

The foregoing quotes from codependent people who are or have been in relationships with sex addicts illustrate thoughts and behaviors that are characteristic of codependency. In the life of most sex addicts there is a person who is engaged in a codependent relationship with him or her. Sometimes these codependent people are perceived as honorable and loyal for staying in difficult relationships or otherwise "putting up with" the acting-out behaviors of the sex addict. Sometimes these codependent people are perceived as foolish or crazy for staying in abusive, destructive, or neglectful relationships. Not until quite recently, however, has it been recognized that people who stay in relationships with sex addicts may be struggling with their *own addiction* in the form of obsessive thinking and compulsive behavior relative to the sex addict.

Simply stated, the object of the codependent person's addiction is another person—an individual and a relationship with that individual that helps to fill a real or perceived need and also helps to shape the codependent person's identity by making him or her feel worthy and acceptable.

Codependent people have the erroneous belief that they can control other people, particularly those people who give them a sense of worth and identity—even if the attention from or relationship with the other person is essentially negative. But because no one can be controlled by another, codependents always have a diversion, always have work to do in their attempts to achieve the impossible. The codependent's efforts to control another person's behavior are compulsive in nature. In fact, many codependents who do leave one relationship with a sex addict often find themselves in a subsequent relationship that is similar in nature and equally painful.

Codependent people also have the erroneous belief that if only they can find the right person, their lives will be perfect and whatever emotional pain they feel will disappear. Typically, codependent people ignore themselves and their needs as they focus on the needs and behaviors of other people.

As any recovering codependent can tell you, codependency is as painful and destructive as other addictions. In fact, the same dynamics seen in other addictions are quite evident in the codependent: compulsive behavior; obsessive thoughts; despair; an intense sense of isolation; powerlessness; a belief that "this time will be different; this time things will work out"; and the struggle to control that which is not subject to control. Codependency shapes and controls people's lives to the extent that sometimes families are abandoned, personal goals are disregarded, opportunities are overlooked, and spiritual growth is undermined. Ultimately, codependency leads to further shame, self-hatred, and loss of self-identity.

Following is the story of a personal struggle with codependency.

Jean's Story:
A Codependent's Struggle

I would hesitate to call my story typical—each codependent's story is unique and, to a great extent, shaped by the sex addict in his or her life. But regardless of the differences between our individual stories, some strikingly similar patterns of behavior and thinking are prominent in all of our stories. These codependent patterns of thinking and behavior made our lives as powerless and unmanageable as the lives of the sex addicts we so desperately—but unsuccessfully— tried to control or change.

My story, like Frank's, is not complete without including the life-transforming component of recovery. A Twelve Step Program helped me understand and accept my partner, myself, and our powerlessness; quite simply, recovery gave me back myself and my life.

As a codependent to a sex addict, my story is also one of pain, loneliness, and acting-out behaviors. For years, I spent so much of my emotional energy looking for just the "right" man—a man who could change my world from the miserable, confused place it was to a place where I would always feel good about myself. As long as I knew that someone desired me sexually, I could accept myself and my world. I felt that sex was the only thing I had to offer a man; I felt "loved" only when someone was sexual with me; and I felt comfortable in a relationship only if sex was its most important element. It was not clear to me at the time, but because my self-worth was based solely on my sexuality, a sex addict was really the "perfect" match for me.

About nine years ago, I met Frank, the man who is now my husband. When we met, I knew that he had a reputation for "sleeping around," even though he was engaged to be married at the time. It seemed to me that we'd be *perfect* together because he'd want to have sex all the time and that, I believed, would make me feel *loved* all the time. I decided that if I could somehow get this man to be sexual with me and *no one else*, I could at last *prove* that I was special. Even as a child, I always longed to be special to someone, anyone. When Frank subsequently broke off his engagement because of his sexual relationship with me, I truly believed that I was then the only woman he was involved with sexually. But even though I was thrilled to know that he wanted me, I was fearful from the beginning of our relationship that sooner or later he would lose interest in me and leave. As a codependent, I essentially was addicted to the sex addict in my life. For this reason, I couldn't bear to think of my life without Frank; I was certain that I'd *die* if he ever left me.

Over the next six years, our sexual acting-out behaviors became more varied, more frequent, and more intense. Even though I had no desire to do many of the things Frank asked me to do, I never felt free to say no to him. I managed to convince myself and my friends that the things we were doing sexually were fun, or trendy, or sophisticated. *I had to justify what I was doing in some way.* I was sure that Frank would act out sexually whether he was with me or not. Knowing this, I decided it was best to always be there with him and try to control the situation to the best of my ability. When he told me that he wanted to include other women in our sexual activities, I suppressed my real feelings and agreed to go along with the idea. Instead of telling him what I *really* thought of the idea, I denied my own needs and instincts and told him I thought it would be interesting and fun to include other people in our sexual activities. But to my way of thinking, I *did* manage to retain some degree of control: I always made sure that the women we invited to share in our sexual activities posed no real threat to me, at least in terms of their appearance. Everywhere we went in those days, I compared myself to other women, and I even "ranked" myself in most situations. If I thought I was the most attractive woman at a party, *I was on top of the world.* But if I thought that another woman at a party was more attractive—particularly to Frank—I'd withdraw from the festivities, then begin a fight with him about some issue completely unrelated to my feelings about the other woman.

I felt distant from Frank, even though we were living together. I was, however, reluctant to acknowledge my feelings about the emotional distance between us; our relationship was so very fragile and I just couldn't rock the boat and risk losing him. Our relationship was based on sex; so as long as I was being sexual with Frank, I knew where he was and what he was feeling. I always felt that it was *my* responsibility to change or to work on whatever was causing problems in our relationship. I was motivated by a belief that if I were prettier, or smarter, or sexier, Frank would love me enough to stay with me and/or to change in the exact ways I wanted him to change. I never trusted him when he was out of my sight, yet I rarely confronted him about my lack of trust in him. It was always less frightening to me if I started a fight with him about an issue that really had nothing at all to do with my feelings about his behavior.

After Frank and I had been together for six years, I felt as if I were dying inside. *I knew that I ought to leave him.* I felt the need for more sharing and more feelings in this relationship; I needed to have someone in my life who I could feel closer to; *I needed to know myself again.* Throughout our relationship, I had given up my own activities and interests just to have time and energy for *him.* I no longer wanted to be sexual with him but I knew if I refused him, our relationship would end forever. In order to cope with this conflict between my feelings and my fear of sharing those feelings, I began to engage in a sort of "passive" acting-out behavior. For example, I'd agree to be sexual with Frank when he asked. I'd then fall asleep, or intentionally think about other things while we were being sexual so that I was not "present" or really aware of what was going on. I simply didn't want to *feel* how meaningless and disconnected our sexual relationship had become.

I could see that I wasn't getting what I wanted from this relationship or from my life, *but I didn't know how to change things.* Then, one day, Frank mentioned a Twelve Step group he had heard about for people with sexual problems; he even talked about joining the group. I felt confused and afraid when I heard him say this, because I had assumed all along that the only real sexual problem he had was his "sleeping around" behavior during the period of time when he was engaged. And as far as I knew, that activity had ended *years* before. So what was going on that I didn't know about? Why did he need to join a group like *that?* All the time I had been with Frank, I labored under the illusion that I could control him. *Now I wondered if I had been wrong.*

The night after Frank's first meeting with a Twelve Step group, we had a big fight. Following that, he went to the phone and called someone in the group. When I overheard him say, "She doesn't know . . . ," I panicked. He got off the phone, sensed my anxiety, and told me that he had been masturbating compulsively for many years. He also told me that there was another Twelve Step group for people in relationships with sex addicts. When I agreed to attend one of these meetings, I felt as though I had agreed to visit another planet! I had absolutely no idea what this group would be like. *I wondered what kind of people actually stayed in relationships with sex addicts.* I expected to encounter crude, immoral people at the meeting, perhaps even characters like those portrayed in porno movies. *But to my surprise, I found at that meeting an intelligent and loving group of people.* As each codependent in the group introduced himself or herself, my anxiety subsided; I felt secure and comfortable with these people. Each of the personal stories shared in the group that evening focused on some common themes that I was all too familiar with: the inability to say no; extreme fear of losing a relationship; feelings of isolation and loneliness within a relationship; subordination of individual needs to the needs of another person; and a persistent feeling that the sex addicts in our lives would stop acting out *if only we* (codependents) *were more attractive, more perfect, more sexually appealing.* As I listened to the stories, I also came to understand that I had acted out my codependency in other relationships in my life, too. Before I met my husband, I often dated men with whom I shared very few interests. But regardless of who I was dating or how few interests we shared, I would routinely abandon my own interests, friends, and studies just to focus all of my energies on the current man in my life.

Early in my recovery, I had some serious doubts about my relationship with Frank, who then had been in my life for almost six years. Eventually, I got in touch with the feelings of anger and resentment I had toward him. I realized that I was uncertain about what our relationship really *was,* other than a sick and destructive mess. In order to collect my feelings and really *confront* them, I moved away for a few months. Time and distance helped both of us see that *despite our addictions, we really liked each other.* We began to discuss marriage. Then, just one week before our official engagement, my husband-to-be told me that he had been sleeping with other women during our relationship; in fact, he admitted that he had been with other women until the time he got into the Program. *I was devastated.* During that period of time, I had assumed I was his only sexual partner—supposedly because I was "the best." Hearing the truth from Frank in this instance was like having the foundation that supported both my identity and my self-worth suddenly ripped out from under me. The members of my Twelve Step group seemed to be the only people who could understand the depth of my pain.

When my emotional pain finally subsided, I could see that I had *always* been powerless over Frank's acting-out behavior. I also realized that he was powerless over his own acting-out behaviors because he was an addict. During the three and a half years I've attended Twelve Step meetings, I have learned to use the Steps in direct relation to my dependence on the sex addict in my life. Now when I look back over my life, I can see how powerless I really *was,* not only in relation to Frank's sexual acting-out behaviors, but also in relation to my own feelings of insecurity. I had learned to be cooperative and conciliatory to the point of being submissive and completely denying my own needs and interests. Now, whenever I find myself wanting to experience the high of that false control again, I remind myself that I learned codependent behavior early in my life and that I am not a bad person for having struggled with codependency. I now have a relationship with my Higher Power who, I believe, was there all along and who got me through those horrible times in the past. Now when I'm fearful about the future, I find that I have to let go and trust that my Higher Power will let me know, through my feelings, what is right for me. I must trust that Frank has a Higher Power too, and that I cannot modify, deter, restrain, or otherwise control his acting-out behaviors.

For me, recovery has meant really *feeling* pain and anger for the first time in my life; recovery has also given me a sense of real joy and intimacy for the first time in my life. My husband and I continue to work on our relationship in recovery with the help of the Twelve Steps and therapy. And I find that as I gain confidence in myself as a person with much more than sex to offer, I am expanding and enriching my life by making time for my own interests, activities, and goals. The early stages of recovery are the toughest. The same Program that promises so much asks us to give up powerful addictive beliefs about ourselves that may have shaped our lives; the Program asks us to love ourselves and believe that we *deserve* love and respect; the Program asks us to look honestly at past behaviors and relationships and reach out for the feelings we have tried to run away from, numb, or deny for so many years. Most important, the Program asks us to let go of trying to understand, analyze, or fix everything and, instead, trust a Higher Power to get us through the process of recovery in our own way and at our own pace. Recovery is never easy, but it is always possible with the help and support of a Higher Power and a Twelve Step Program. My road to recovery has been a rough one, but it's getting easier all the time.

Questions To Consider

The questions that follow reflect thought and behavior patterns that are common to codependents in their relationships with sex addicts. These questions do not constitute a standardized test or inventory designed to identify or evaluate codependency. These questions do, however, serve as a point of reference for people who are (or have been) in relationships with sex addicts. Affirmative responses to a number of these questions suggest that a person's thoughts and behaviors are similar to the thoughts and behaviors of people who are codependent to sex addicts. Those concerned about codependent patterns in their lives are encouraged to seek help through a Twelve Step Program.

☐ 1. Do you sense that your thoughts and/or behaviors relative to your partner and your relationship with him or her are causing problems in your life?

☐ 2. Have thoughts about your relationship with your partner interfered with your ability to function at work or at school?

☐ 3. Do you fail to meet commitments or fail to carry out responsibilities because of your relationship?

☐ 4. Do you struggle to control or completely stop certain thoughts or behaviors related to your partner and your relationship with him or her?

☐ 5. Do you focus on your partner and your relationship with him or her in order to escape, deny, or numb your feelings?

☐ 6. Do you think about your partner more or less than you would like to?

☐ 7. Have you taken financial risks with your own resources by giving or loaning your partner money for his or her sexual activities?

☐   8. Does it seem as though there is another person or force inside of you that drives you to get into or stay in relationships?

☐   9. Do you have two standards of fidelity—one for yourself and one for your partner/spouse?

☐   10. Do you think you would be happy if only you could give your partner enough sex and/or just the right kind of sex?

☐   11. Do you feel empty or shameful after having sexual fantasies or engaging in sexual activities with your partner?

☐   12. Do you feel obligated to have sex?

☐   13. Have you ever promised yourself that you would never again have another sexual relationship?

☐   14. Do you find it necessary to fantasize or distract yourself in some way during sexual activity?

☐   15. Do you dress in such a way as to make your body appear undesirable?

☐   16. Do you set rules regarding when, how, or with whom you can be sexual, then break those rules?

☐   17. Do you focus on your relationship in order to deal with, deny, or avoid problems in your life?

☐   18.ˋ Does your partner use threats or promises in order to have sexual activity with you?

☐   19. Do you sometimes find yourself flirting with someone or being sexual with someone and wondering how it happened?

☐   20. Have you stayed in a marriage or other relationship only because you thought that no one else would want you?

☐   21. Do you think that your sexual abilities are the most important qualities you have to offer another person?

☐   22. Do you dread or fear trips out of town because of what you think your partner might do sexually while you're away?

☐ 23. When you have child care responsibilities, do you put a higher priority on your partner than you do on the welfare of the child(ren) in your care?

☐ 24. Does your relationship interfere with your spiritual or religious life? Does your behavior in your relationship cause you to believe that you don't deserve to have a religious or spiritual life?

☐ 25. Have you sought medical attention for injuries related to your sexual activities?

☐ 26. Are you afraid to leave your partner alone with children, for fear that sexual contact might take place?

☐ 27. Has your relationship ever led you to consider suicide or self-mutilation?

☐ 28. When you are in a relationship with someone, do you try to make sure that another sex partner will be available to you, in case anything goes wrong with the first relationship?

☐ 29. Do you spend time with or have sex with people you don't even like or respect because you feel it is better than being alone?

☐ 30. Do you stay in unsatisfying, painful, humiliating, neglectful, disrespectful or otherwise unhealthy relationships only so that you can continue to be sexual with someone?

☐ 31. Are you unhappy or uncomfortable with your partner's need for sex or the nature of the sexual behavior he or she desires?

☐ 32. Are you afraid to say no to sex with your partner? Are you afraid to refuse to participate in certain sexual activities with him or her?

☐ 33. Do you consent to have sex with your partner even when you are ill or otherwise not feeling well?

☐ 34. Do you either minimize or exaggerate the facts when discussing your sexual life with others?

☐   35. Does your partner initiate sexual activity with you before you are awake?

☐   36. Do you have chronic medical problems with your sex organs?

☐   37. Do you jeopardize your own safety and/or health by not taking reasonable precautions or by going to unsafe places in order to please your partner?

☐   38. Have you lost a job or risked losing a job because of your preoccupation with a relationship?

☐   39. Does your relationship cause you to violate your ethical standards, principles, and/or the oaths of your profession?

☐   40. Do you scan printed material (novels, newspapers, magazines) so that you can find and then hide or dispose of the things that you think might sexually stimulate your partner?

☐   41. Have you been injured due to the frequency, intensity, or nature of sexual activity you participate in with your partner?

☐   42. Have your sexual behaviors led to hospitalization?

☐   43. Do your sexual behaviors with your partner lead you to risk injury, illness, or death?

☐   44. Do you feel compelled to dress a certain way or to take part in certain rituals in order to be sexual with your partner?

☐   45. Have you thrown out or destroyed your partner's collection of sexually explicit materials (magazines, films, videos)?

A Message From The Authors

We have shared our personal experiences in this book in an effort to help all people understand a serious, life-threatening problem that is often obscured by misunderstanding and controversy. If you know someone who you think may have problems and/or questions related to sex addiction or codependency, tell them about this book and please tell them also that they are not alone: *help is available.*

In order to provide some guidance for additional help, we have adapted and also quoted some passages from the book *Hope & Recovery/A Twelve Step guide for healing from compulsive sexual behavior,* (CompCare, 1987):

• People seeking help for sexual addiction and/or codependency through a Twelve Step Program need to *be persistent.* Because of the anonymous nature of the Program, as well as a public relations policy based on attraction rather than promotion, many people find that it requires some effort to obtain specific information about Twelve Step programs. "In their searches for help, many people have found it useful to refer to a phone book, or to consult with a social service agency or a community mental health referral service for information regarding anonymous groups based on the Twelve Step Program."

• Even though awareness is growing and there are currently Twelve Step groups for sex addicts and codependents throughout the country, not all communities have specialized groups of this kind. "People who are unable to find Twelve Step groups for sex addicts and codependents are encouraged to attend other Twelve Step group meetings and to consult with people there about establishing special Twelve Step groups to address the needs of sex addicts and codependents."

- People who find that there are several Twelve Step groups for sex addicts and codependents in their communities are encouraged to attend as many different meetings as they choose to attend. But "it is important that they select one of these meetings to attend regularly so they will have an opportunity to get to know the people there."

- "When people do find and attend Twelve Step group meetings suited to their needs, they are encouraged to ask questions—lots of them—and to feel free about asking recovering addicts in groups to share their stories—the nature of their acting-out behaviors; the event, situation, or feeling that finally led them to seek help; how they set their boundaries and continue to monitor them; ways they are different now; and how they continue to grow in their recovery."

- "Above all, those who are seeking help are encouraged to be patient and gentle with themselves and to remember that there are people in the Twelve Step fellowship who understand what they are going through and who will care about them and give them support every step of the way."

Recommended Reading

The following works are recommended by both sex addicts and codependents to sex addicts:

Anonymous. *Alcoholics Anonymous.* New York: A.A. World Services. 1976 (©1939). Referred to as the "Big Book," this is the first and basic work on the Twelve Steps—what they are and how they work. Includes stories of the Twelve Steps working in the lives of recovering people.

Beattie, Melody. *Codependent No More.* Center City: Hazelden. 1987. This look at the life-affecting aspects of codependency offers guidance for codependents who have forgotten how to take care of themselves.

Carnes, Patrick. *Contrary to Love: Helping the Sexual Addict.* Minneapolis: CompCare Publishers. 1989. Detailed descriptions and definitions trace the origins and consequences of sex addiction and codependency. For therapists as well as addicts and codependents.

_____ . *Out of the Shadows: Understanding Sexual Addiction.* Minneapolis: CompCare Publishers. 1983. Landmark work that first identified and defined sex addiction illustrates how recovery is possible through therapy and an adapted use of the Twelve Steps of A.A.

Grateful Members (Anonymous). *The Twelve Steps for Everyone . . . who really wants them.* Minneapolis: CompCare Publishers. 1977 (©1975). Guide for life and growth features paths to emotional and spiritual health based on the Twelve Steps.

Halpern, Howard. *How to Break Your Addiction to a Person.* New York: Bantam. 1982. Describes the characteristics of addictive relationships and outlines specific ways to make positive changes.

Hunter, Mic. *Abused Boys: The Neglected Victims of Sexual Abuse.* Lexington, Massachusetts: Lexington Books. 1989. Describes effects of sexual abuse on male victims as children and as adults. Includes first-person accounts by men abused as children.

Hunter, Mic. *What Is Sex Addiction?* Center City: Hazelden Foundation. 1988. Leaflet briefly introduces some of the characteristics of sex addiction.

Hunter, Mic and "Jem." *The First Step for People in Relationships with Sex Addicts.* Minneapolis: CompCare Publishers. 1989. Collaborative effort by a professional therapist and an anonymous recovering codependent. Guides codependents through questions designed to help them acknowledge the origins, effects, and realities of powerlessness and unmanageability in their lives.

Paul, Drs. Jordan and Margaret. *Do I Have to Give Up Me to Be Loved by You?* Minneapolis: CompCare Publishers. 1983. Provides ways to handle conflict in relationships that bring intimacy with your partner, as well as personal growth and strength for you.

P.D.N.E.C. (Anonymous). *Hope and Recovery: A Twelve Step guide for healing from compulsive sexual behavior.* Minneapolis: CompCare Publishers. 1987. The personal stories of Frank and Jean that you have just read were first published in *Hope and Recovery,* along with first person stories of seventeen recovering sex addicts. Applies the Twelve Step Program of Alcoholics Anonymous to the problem of sex addiction. Chapters 1-18 of *Hope and Recovery* are also available on audio cassette.

Peele, Stanton. *Love and Addiction.* New York: New American Library. 1975. An examination of relationships using the addiction model.

Schneider, Jennifer P., M.D. *Back from Betrayal.* San Francisco: Harper/Hazelden. 1988. Identifies the problem of multiple extramarital affairs as an addiction and offers hope and advice for women who act as sexual codependents in their relationships with their husbands and lovers.